STUDIES IN ENGLISH LITERATURE No. 26

General Editor

David Daiches

Professor of English in the School of English and American Studies,
University of Sussex

To William

WILLIAM SHAKESPEARE:
THE WINTER'S TALE

by

A. D. NUTTALL

Professor of English Literature
University of Sussex

EDWARD ARNOLD

15,418

© A. D. NUTTALL 1966

First published 1966
by
Edward Arnold (Publishers) Ltd
25 Hill Street, London W1X 8LL

Reprinted 1970, 1974

ISBN 0 7131 5103 X

Printed in Great Britain by
The Camelot Press Ltd., London and Southampton

General Preface

The object of this series is to provide studies of individual novels, plays and groups of poems and essays which are known to be widely read by students. The emphasis is on clarification and evaluation; biographical and historical facts, while they may be discussed when they throw light on particular elements in a writer's work, are generally subordinated to critical discussion. What kind of work is this? What exactly goes on here? How good is this work, and why? These are the questions that each writer will try to answer.

It should be emphasized that these studies are written on the assumption that the reader has already read carefully the work discussed. The objective is not to enable students to deliver opinions about works they have not read, nor is it to provide ready-made ideas to be applied to works that have been read. In one sense all critical interpretation can be regarded as foisting opinions on readers, but to accept this is to deny the advantages of any sort of critical discussion directed at students or indeed at anybody else. The aim of these studies is to provide what Coleridge called in another context 'aids to reflection' about the works discussed. The interpretations are offered as suggestive rather than as definitive, in the hope of stimulating the reader into developing further his own insights. This is after all the function of all critical discourse among sensible people.

DAVID DAICHES

Acknowledgements

I should like to thank my colleagues, Laurence Lerner and Gabriel Josipovici, for reading and commenting on my manuscript.

All references to works of Shakespeare other than *The Winter's Tale* are according to W. J. Craig's three volume Oxford edition of 1911–12. All references to *The Winter's Tale* are according to the Arden Edition of J. H. P. Pafford, 4th edition, 1963.

The author and publishers wish to acknowledge the kind permission given by Methuen & Co., Ltd. to reprint an extract from *Shakespeare's Wordplay* by M. M. Mahood; the editor and The Nonesuch Press to reprint an extract from "A Descriptive Catalogue" in *Prose and Poetry of William Blake*, edited by Sir Geoffrey Keynes; and Harcourt, Brace and World, Inc. to reprint an extract from *Fables of Identity* by Northrop Frye.

A. D. NUTTALL

Contents

1. Introductory

The Winter's Tale is the most beautiful play Shakespeare ever wrote. It is a less intelligent play than *Hamlet* (but not *much* less intelligent). It is less profound than *King Lear* (but not *much* less). It is not (as some readers will already have begun to conclude) a pretty play, of 'merely aesthetic' appeal. For it is far less elegant than *Love's Labour's Lost* and much more disturbing than *A Midsummer Night's Dream*. The beauty of *The Winter's Tale* does not so much charm the eye as pierce the viscera. It does not divert the spectator; it turns him inside out. But the days when critics could be found to stigmatise the play as a tissue of superficially pleasing imagery are long past. Lytton Strachey published in 1922 a famous essay in which he argued that *The Winter's Tale*, like the other last plays, was written by a man tired of life, tired of everything but poetry. Since that year verbal punishment of Strachey has become a regular pastime of Shakespearean critics. Strachey was wrong and the critics were right, and it no longer seems necessary to recapitulate their arguments. Rather, I am concerned to combat a subtler heresy, a heresy from which Strachey, immersed in his grosser error, was entirely free. My quarry is the critical doctrine, never explicitly stated but implicit in much post-Strachey criticism, that the only way to defend the play against a charge of superficiality is to rearrange it as a metaphysical system: the doctrine that if Lytton Strachey is wrong, Wilson Knight or S. L. Bethell must be right.

The Winter's Tale belongs to the strange last phase of Shakespeare's writing life. It is closely associated, in time and in *genre*, with *Pericles*, *Cymbeline* and *The Tempest*; that is to say, it is one of the group of plays which Coleridge termed the Romances. These plays conform to a loose Elizabethan definition of comedy in that the principal persons of the drama, though they may fall into great distress, are ultimately spared for a happy ending in love and reunion. Thus it is perfectly fair to call them comedies: the placing of *Cymbeline* with the tragedies in the 1623 Folio must have been due to some editorial accident. The reason why most critics and commentators have been unwilling to rest content with the designation 'comedy' is that without being actually inaccurate it fails to convey any hint of what is distinctive about these plays. The ways in which *The Tempest* differs from *A Midsummer Night's Dream* have proved vastly more interesting than the ways in which it resembles it. A term was needed sufficiently comprehensive to cover all four plays, sufficiently narrow to exclude the rest of the comedies. 'Romance', though it may seem almost as loose a word as 'comedy', has proved useful by becoming a quasi-technical term, much like the term 'metaphysical' in its special application to the Metaphysical Poets. Both 'romance' and 'metaphysical' hold some degree of descriptive validity, but their real usefulness lies in their being a sort of proper noun or family name rather than in their descriptive power. There is a sense in which the last plays of Shakespeare are *sui generis*, so that any word would do (the blanker the better). In the first place the Romances are united by a preoccupation with a common story-pattern. In them people joined by some love-relation of blood or marriage are at first separated, usually in a storm, but in the end, beyond all expectation, are brought together again; he that was lost is found, she that was thought to be dead proves warm and living. This pattern of loss and renewal is dwelt on with a peculiar kind of imaginative depth not found in the earlier comedies. The effect of this special concentration is in a manner to isolate the recurring pattern and to give it a special, mythical force of its own. It ceases to be just 'What happened to Hermione and Leontes' and becomes instead a sort of progress of love. It may be objected that this special sense of the myth as prior to the individuals who perform it could come only to one who had read all four Romances and had mentally placed them together. The story-pattern (allowing for variations) is common to all four plays; the characters are each peculiar to his or her own particular play; hence, and hence only, can we separate the myth from the individual characters. This may be so. But I suspect that the perusal of a single play would yield the same intuition of myth. Rosalind in *As You Like It* speaks with the voice of Rosalind. Hermione in *The Winter's Tale* speaks with the voice of Alcestis, of Persephone and Eurydice. Further, it is not so much that the story-pattern of *The Winter's Tale* reminds one of the story-pattern of *Cymbeline*. Rather, it evokes in a peculiarly powerful way all the fairy tales one ever heard, at a time of life when 'and they lived happily ever after' could still focus a kind of imaginative passion in the hearer; it suggests what it would be like to watch Spring following upon Winter, as if for the first time. Finally, it has a strange property which I can only come at by a feeble epigram which will be meaningful to some, fatuous to others: the play seems to remind one of itself. This strange reverberation depends on an apprehension of immediate diversity being followed by an intuition of identity. Thus Hermione is Hermione and yet has a strange radiance which suggests someone else standing behind her, speaking through her. As I have said, she suggests Alcestis, who went freely into hell to save her husband from the revengeful shades, resolving his disease by her death. So far we have only the diversity without which the imaginative 'reverberation' could not begin at all. But this feeling is closely followed by an intuition that Alcestis is not the 'meaning' of Hermione; Alcestis and Hermione are rather the same person. To say that Hermione suggests Alcestis is not at all like saying that Hermione suggests, e.g. 'harmony' (though she may do this too).

It is of course easy, fatally easy, for a critic to be drawn into folly by this property of mythic reverberation. He senses that the story is not 'What happened to Leontes and Hermione', but something more. Accordingly he cries 'Allegory!' and begins filling in the vacuum in his scheme of significations with the nearest materials. Bethell, with some excuse, drew on Christianity. Wilson Knight drew on his own very indulgent metaphysic. A parallel case is the reception of Kafka's novels. *The Trial*, the criticis perceived (correctly), is not just a story about a fellow who was tried. So, they concluded (incorrectly) that it must be an allegory of e.g. Marxism or e.g. Christianity. This is the 'subtler heresy' to which I am opposed.

To allegorise a play into a metaphysical system is to smooth off its corners. Consciously or unconsciously, the critic who has decided that *The Winter's Tale* is an allegory will omit idiosyncrasies of character, freaks of imagery. In recent years a rich vocabulary has grown up, enabling such critics to rationalise this inhibition of natural vigilance. We have learned that the Jacobean theatre was not naturalistic but ritual, that what we take for individuals are really walking 'conventions'. The arguments advanced to support these propositions tend to be exactly half-valid and no more. For example it is perfectly true that the Jacobean theatre is non-naturalistic in that its persons speak in verse. Anyone who concluded from reading a Jacobean play that the men of that age habitually talked in verse in the street would be wrong. But then no one ever did so conclude. On the other hand it is plainly false to claim that there are no characters in Shakespeare's plays.

Many things happens in Shakespeare's plays which do not happen in nineteenth century novels. But this does not mean that Shakespeare, through some prohibition of the *Zeitgeist*, was unable to elaborate individual human beings every bit as distinctive as any we find in the pages of Henry James. There is something viciously aprioristic about an advance decision to avert the eyes from any manifestation of psychological idiosyncrasy. The fact that an atmosphere of myth permeates *The Winter's Tale* does not license the critic to relax his vigilance. All I ask is that we give to *The Winter's Tale* as fine a degree of attention as we extend to any of our fellow human beings in ordinary conversation. Our sensibilities must not become specialised instruments for picking up elements of the 'Elizabethan World Picture' or the Doctrine of Redemption and channelling off everything else. We must be as receptive to the dense variety of the play as we are to our friends. A great poet working with quasi-mythical materials is properly the object, not of a lowered, but a heightened consciousness. The harder one looks at Shakespeare, the better he gets.

2. Sicilia: Jealousy and Guilt

Like many of Shakespeare's other plays, *The Winter's Tale* opens with a short scene of expository dialogue from minor characters. Two courtiers, Camillo and Archidamus, enter, chatting about their respective sovereigns, Leontes and Polixenes. They discuss, in language of high courtesy, the rooted affection between the two kings, who were educated together as children. Polixenes, we learn, is staying with Leontes, and it is likely that Leontes will return his visit in the coming summer. Further, we are told that Leontes has a son, Mamillius, who is the delight and admiration of all who see him. The whole scene is over in a few minutes, and it is easy to forget that the play opens, not with the kings, but with the courtiers. In precisely the same way people tend to forget that *King Lear* begins, not with the aged king dividing his kingdom, but with the conversation between Kent and Gloucester. Shakespeare likes to linger a little on the edge of his drama before he goes to the heart of the matter by bringing on his procession of principals. Of course the device allows him to fill in preliminary information, but there would have been no technical difficulty, in the case of *The Winter's Tale*, in doing this without the opening dialogue. The truth is perhaps that Shakespeare wishes to alert his audience slowly rather than instantaneously, to give them the variation in a minor key before they hear it in the major.

Camillo and Archidamus, while they describe their sovereigns, also speak like echoes of them. They exchange civilities on the pattern of their masters. The mutual love of Leontes and Polixenes is half mirrored, half parodied in the courtiers' conversation—

Archidamus. . . . our entertainment shall shame us: we will be justified in our loves: for indeed—
Camillo. Beseech you—
Archidamus. Verily I speak it in the freedom of my knowledge: we cannot with such magnificence—in so rare—I know not what to say—We will give you sleepy drinks, that your senses (unintelligent of our insufficience) may, though they cannot praise us, as little accuse us.

Camillo.   You pay a great deal too dear for what's given freely.
                                                                (I. i. 8-18)

Note that the sentiments they express are in a way more appropriate
to their masters than themselves. Archidamus apologises in advance for
the inadequate hospitality Bohemia will extend to Sicilia, but adds that
sincerity of affection must make up for material insufficiency. Camillo
murmurs polite deprecation. Archidamus in a little fever of courtesy
(here we see the parody element) insists on his point. Camillo counters
by suggesting that discrepancies of material hospitality are entirely
irrelevant in a free exchange of loves. Yet it is evident that it is not
Archidamus' responsibility to determine the munificence of the projected
entertainment, any more than his personal affection for Camillo is
competent to make good its deficiences. In the description of the childhood friendship of Leontes and Polixenes ('. . . trained together in their
childhoods, and there rooted betwixt them such an affection which
cannot choose but branch now') there is a hint of the imagery of natural
growth which is to permeate the play. At the point where Archidamus
turns the conversation to Mamillius, the tone, as the Arden editor notes,
becomes more direct and straightforward. The audience finds itself
listening with a different kind of seriousness, as it is told how the young
prince makes the sick healthy, the old as if they were young again.
Camillo and Archidamus are a courtly reflection of Leontes and
Polixenes. The poetry in which the name of Mamillius moves is something more mysterious; to vary the metaphor we could say that the
passage is a pre-echo of the play to follow, in which the children help
to restore the parents. Of course all this echoing and pre-echoing would
not be likely to occur in a realistic novel. It is a good example of the sort
of feature poetic drama does *not* share with later naturalism. This opening
scene is slight but deft. The pessimists in the audience, and also the
inveterate theatre-goers who are used to the way dramatists disrupt a
first act *status quo*, will perhaps have their first intuition of unease before
it is over; they will smell *hubris* in the complacency of such observations
as 'I think there is not in the world either malice or matter to alter it'
(I. i. 33). But the greater part of the audience will apprehend nothing but
happiness and love.

    The next scene is the second most important in the play (the most
important is IV. iv). It begins with Polixenes' taking an elaborate leave
of his hosts. Leontes and Hermione, with competing extravagances of

courtesy, press him to prolong his stay. Polixenes successfully resists
Leontes but yields to Hermione, who teasingly urges him to describe to
her his childhood friendship with Leontes. He replies in lines of a
crystalline poetry, that it was a period of sunlit, timeless innocence. A
little later Leontes is readmitted to the conversation, and congratulates
his wife on her success in persuasion. So far nothing has happened to
discredit the picture drawn by Archidamus and Camillo in the first
scene. But in a few lines everything is changed. Leontes ('*aside*') begins
a kind of muttering, rambling speech which reveals that his attitude to
Polixenes is in fact poisoned by a pathological, disabling jealousy. He
calls the young prince Mamillius to him and scans his features for
evidence of his paternity. The speeches he addresses to Mamillius are
extremely poignant, because Mamillius so nearly succeeds in saving
his father from his inwardly erupting delusion. It is as if Camillo's
description of him as life-giving had a more serious accuracy than
Camillo himself knew. There is one moment when Leontes notices a
smudge on the little boy's nose, and another where his attention is
caught by his sky-blue eye. These may sound trivial occurrences, but
when it is understood that they represent the sole intrusions of objective reality upon a diseased soul, they will assume their proper status.
In particular, the second moment

> Look on me with your welkin eye (I. ii. 136)

holds one of the most beautiful images in the play. The sudden association
of the child's eye with the sky has the effect of a fresh wind, after the
claustrophobic fetor of Leontes' spiritual imprisonment. But the in-
fluence of Mamillius is intermittent only. Leontes relapses into his strange
jealousy and, when Hermione approaches him in enquiring solicitude,
controls himself with difficulty. The conversation begins to run again on
children. Polixenes, describing his own son, stresses once more the
therapeutic properties which infancy holds for maturity—

> He makes a July's day short as December;
> And with his varying childness cures in me
> Thoughts that would thick my blood. (I. ii. 169-71)

The lines fall with a special weight, partly because of their (presumably
unconscious) diagnostic accuracy, partly through the resonant imagery
of the seasons. Leontes, with what may be a wholly genuine effort of
objectivity, asserts—'So stands this squire/Officed with me'—but there

is a facetiousness in the language which contrasts with Polixenes' warmth and makes us doubt whether the effort was successful. At all events, Leontes is unable to keep up a show of reasonable good humour for long, and soon makes an excuse to walk on one side with Mamillius. Once apart from the rest, he can give himself up once more to jealous soliloquising and prurient observation of his wife's behaviour with Polixenes. The rest of the scene is taken up, first with Leontes' instructing Camillo to murder Polixenes, then with Camillo's disclosure of these instructions to Polixenes, and their precipitate flight.

Such is the scene in the barest outline. Of course, such a summary leaves a great deal unsaid. There is some temptation to describe the opening courtesy-combat as a sort of formal minuet. But it is a temptation which should be resisted. If we compare this episode with, say, the wit-combats of *Love's Labour's Lost* we shall see at once how acutely naturalistic *The Winter's Tale* episode is. The whole conversation is veined with a kind of nervous tension which continually reminds us of the complex human personalities lying behind the *personae* of manners. This psychological stress is by no means without parallel in the Romances. Act II, Scene i of *The Tempest* exhibits tensions of a similar order. A good Shakespearean should be able to 'hear' the naturalistic quality of this dialogue almost from the start. How this perception is conveyed is not easy to demonstrate, but perhaps the *timing* of the lines has much to do with it. Take the conversation between Camillo and Leontes at I. ii. 321f.:

Camillo. . . . but I cannot
      Believe this crack to be in my dread mistress
      (So sovereignly being honourable).
      I have loved thee,——
Leontes.   Make that thy question, and go rot!

Leontes' angry reply means, as the Arden editor says, 'If you are going to doubt that, go to blazes', and refers, not to Camillo's last remark, but to his previous expression of loyalty to Hermione. The extreme naturalism of this can be verified with a concealed tape-recorder. Such dialogue, more realistic than logical, is a polar opposite to the sort of rhyming stichomythia we find in early Shakespeare.

Thus the eruption of Leontes' jealousy is a shock, but somehow, not a total shock. It persistently 'feels realistic'. Its apparently gratuitous inception has caused commentators a good deal of brain-searching. Those who are offended by the want of motivation can be neatly answered out of Aristotle. There is a passage in *The Poetics* (1450b) which tells us that we perceive a person's ethical character when he makes an 'unobvious decision'. This is best illustrated by an example. Suppose I am about to cross the road when I see a car coming. I carefully step back until it has gone by. In this situation I made a decision (to step back), but it was a perfectly obvious one. It tells you nothing about my ethical character. Suppose, on the other hand, a man comes to the door and asks for five shillings; I kick him down the steps. Here again I made a decision, but this time it was not at all obvious what to do; and you have learned a great deal about my character. One may thus formulate a law of dramatic composition: the depth of ethical character in a given person is in inverse proportion to his external motivation. The application of all this to Leontes is simple. If we supply him with the sort of good reason for jealousy some ·critics seem to want, he instantly ceases to be (what he certainly should be in the first part of the play) a villain. Coleridge really saw this when he contrasted the elaborately motivated jealousy of Othello with the 'fishing jealousies'[1] of Leontes. Indeed, the example of *Othello* is a useful one, since it not only provides us with a contrast to Leontes, in Othello, but an analogue, in Iago. For Iago's hatred of the Moor, as for Leontes' jealousy of Polixenes, there seems to be no solid reason. Yet if the play made it unequivocally clear that Othello *had*, for example, seduced Iago's wife, this provision of a solid motive would forthwith abolish Iago's peculiar depth of wickedness. Part of the trouble with Webster's tragedies is that the concatenation of motive is too invariably complete. When X poisons Y it is always because Y has previously murdered X's mistress, Z, and so on. Thus we do not find in Webster that incalculable depth of evil and good which we find in Shakespeare's characters. Instead we receive the impression of a generalised evil, of a corrupt society.

Note that all this applies to what we may call 'public motivation' only. Thus, we have been concerned with the sort of motive referred to in statements like 'Othello murdered Desdemona because Iago convinced him that she was false' rather than with the very different kind of statement: 'Othello murdered Desdemona because of a sense of his own inadequacy.' The second sort of statement really deals with a different

---

[1] *Shakespearean Criticism*, ed. T. M. Raysor, 2nd edn. (1960), vol. I, p. 113.

order of causality, though this is not always noticed. Thus A. C. Bradley thought he was disagreeing with Coleridge when he argued[1] that Iago does have a motive—in his hatred for Othello's goodness. But all that Coleridge needed for his thesis was that Iago (and Leontes) should have no good, public reason. The analogy between Iago and Leontes holds only at the level of public motivation. As soon as we turn to the private level the immense difference between them is evident.

Bradley's transference of attention from the public to the inward world warns us that the neat Aristotelian resolution of our difficulties, though competent within its own limits, does not exhaust the possibilities of dramatic psychology. We have seen enough to realise that the abruptness of Leontes' emotion, so far from being awkwardly artificial, is really close to the apparent capriciousness of real life. It is only in works of fiction that everyone has a good reason for everything he does. But, in real life, though actions may not have a justification, they tend at least to have an explanation. Where we can see no good reason for a man's action, we tend, in fact, to look for a *psychological* explanation.

Is the jealousy of Leontes as devoid of psychological credibility as it is of reason? As soon as we stop looking for 'solid, external motivation' and put on our psychological spectacles we shall see that the character of Leontes is far less of a vacuum than we had supposed. J. I. M. Stewart in his *Character and Motive in Shakespeare* (1949)[2] offered a Freudian interpretation: the jealousy of Leontes is pathological; it arises through the projection of guilt proper to Leontes himself upon the very person before whom he is most ashamed;[3] Hermione is a standing reproach to his conscience, therefore she must be daubed with slime; but Leontes is not propelled into the truly delusional phrase until his condition is brought to a crisis by the arrival of the great love, and the great guilt, of his life—Polixenes; the presence of Polixenes is a torment from which the only refuge is neurosis; finally, there is an element of genuine sexuality (which Leontes' hungry vigilance succeeds in picking up) in the courtesy of Hermione to Polixenes; social conventions do not merely simulate non-existent emotions; they also transmute and accommodate pressures which might otherwise be dangerous; in allowing a degree of flirtatiousness they act as a 'safety-valve' for something quite real.

[1] *Shakespearean Tragedy*, 2nd edn. (1905), pp. 209-30.
[2] pp. 33-37.
[3] See Freud, *Collected Papers* (1924), vol. II, pp. 232f. (cited by Stewart).

The reader who is sceptical (as it is quite right to be sceptical) of Freudian theory may be surprised to learn how much support for this particular interpretation can be extracted from the text. Let us take the points one by one.

First the thesis that Leontes' attitude to Hermione is a disguised projection of his own guilt: this notion was in fact put forward long before Freud's theories reached England. At line 235 of this scene Leontes says to Camillo

> I have trusted thee, Camillo,
> With all the nearest things to my heart, as well
> My chamber-counsels, wherein, priest-like, thou
> Hast cleans'd my bosom: I from thee departed
> Thy penitent reform'd.

On this Furness, writing still in the nineteenth century, commented

> Sufficient importance has not been given to the full meaning of this passage . . . These *private chamber-councils* involved no questions of state, or government, but were concerned with the private life of Leontes, with impure deeds from which the bosom of Leontes should be cleansed, and for which he should repent, and depart a penitent. This reference to the past life of Leontes, brings his character into harmony with what is known to experts in Mental Diseases, that those patients who are victims of sudden attacks of insane jealousy are, at times, not free from the reproach which they insanely ascribe to the objects of their suspicion.[1]

The projection theory is here, complete. The evidence, admittedly, is slender. Yet the note of Leontes' personal guilt is struck, and at II. i. 52, lest we should have forgotten, it is struck again.

There Leontes demands how it came about that the gates were opened to the fugitives, Polixenes and Camillo. A lord explains how this divergence from the proper order of things went through as it had often gone through before—Camillo, claiming to be acting on orders from Leontes, had the gates opened. Enough is said to make it clear that the opening of the gates after locking-up time was something irregular. That the lord's reference to previous occasions is in some way discreditable to Leontes is apparent from his reply—'I know't too well.' His righteous indignation is suddenly, and oddly, abated.

Leontes' allusion to his long-standing practice of confessing to Camillo

[1] Variorum Edition, p. 43.

has just the context which a theory of projected jealousy would require. He is importuning Camillo to confirm his judgement of Hermione. In effect, he says: 'Do you not see that this evil is present in Hermione; can I not trust you; have I not confessed to you again and again?' The transition from Hermione's guilt to his own is as fluid as Freud could have wished. He plainly thinks of the disclosure he is about to make concerning Hermione as analogous to his own previous confessions.

Next, we have to deal with the suggestion that Leontes' outburst, while generally connected with his own past errors, is specifically connected with Polixenes.

We may note, to begin with, that the play sets our minds moving by presenting us with a curious, and abrupt, correlation. The growth of Leontes' strange jealousy *coincides* with the visit of his dearest friend. To plot the coincidence a little more precisely, Leontes' jealousy erupts at the emotionally laden moment of parting from this friend. The human intelligence, faced with a coincidence, naturally tries to transform it into a causal relation; we grow suspicious, and hunt for clues to a possible connexion between the coincident phenomena. Now in the present instance it appears that Shakespeare has not only given us the correlation but has left a trail of clues as well. These 'clues' take the form of the merest innuendo, and the reader must estimate for himself the weight of inference which they may properly be called upon to bear. The sequence of innuendo works (if I am not mistaken) by first stressing the special strength of the attachment between Leontes and Polixenes, and the associating it with sexuality.

In the first expository scene we saw Archidamus and Camillo raising the question whether malice could touch this great love, only to reject the possibility out of hand: 'I think there is not in the world either malice or matter to alter it' (I. i. 33-34). The imputation is denied but the question has existed for an instant in our minds. Innocence is as often lost with the raising as with the answering of questions. Certainly the denial of Archidamus does not kill the question. It rises to the surface again in the following scene, teasingly but persistently. Interestingly, it is Hermione who plays the Devil's Advocate, by treating Polixenes as her sexual rival. Of course, her speeches are playful. But all the smiles and laughter fail to numb the nervous tension which is present in the conversation even before Leontes' first outburst. At line 60 she begins to probe the boyhood relationship of Leontes and Polixenes:

Hermione.   Come, I'll question you
                Of my lord's tricks, and yours, when you were boys.
                You were pretty lordings then?
Polixenes.   We were, fair queen,
                Two lads that thought there was no more behind,
                But such a day to-morrow as to-day,
                And to be boy eternal.

Quietly, but unmistakably, a word like 'tricks' contrasts with the marvellous imagery of innocence in Polixenes' reply. And Hermione refuses to be drawn from her attitude of insinuating levity:

Hermione.   Was not my lord
                The verier wag o' th' two? (I. ii. 65-66)

This time Polixenes makes a special effort, and explicitly rejects the suggestion of vice. He speaks intently to her of their lamb-like innocence, stresses that they did not know what evil was, and adds

                        Had we pursu'd that life,
                And our weak spirits ne'er been higher rear'd
                With stronger blood, we should have answer'd heaven
                Boldly 'not guilty', the imposition clear'd
                Hereditary ours. (I. ii. 71-75)

I do not know whether a contemporary audience would have detected a note of hysteria in this claim to have been exempt from Original Sin. Even if we decide that they would not, and that the speech is a simple example of hyperbole, we are still left with the question, 'Why does Shakespeare put *this particular* hyperbole into the mouth of Polixenes? Why does he, at this point, drop into our minds the sin which drove man from the Garden of Eden?' Certainly, Hermione refuses to be impressed—

                        By this we gather
                You have tripp'd since.

Her search for peccadilloes has something relentless about it. Polixenes reacts with a strange mixture of accusation and gallantry—purity was easy as long as they were not tempted by their future wives. Hermione's reply, 'Grace to boot!' has exercised the commentators. The Arden editor is surely wrong in paraphrasing 'What next indeed!' The Oxford English Dictionary does better with 'Grace be my helper!' Hermione gives this exclamation on finding herself classified as a temptation. The tables are turned on her in the courtesy-skirmish. The whole exchange composes a sort of antiphonal song on the theme of Polixenes and Leontes. Polixenes bears the major part, Hermione the parodying undersong. Critics have listened only to Polixenes. We may remember all this, when, a little later in the scene, Hermione and Polixenes cross the stage to Leontes and ask him what is affecting him so strangely. Leontes' reply is very curious; he says (lines 153-60) that he was thinking of his childhood. It is hard to account for this reply, unless, with one part of his mind, he *was*. The theory that his jealousy is a cloak for guilt felt at a childhood love has at least the merit of placing all these apparently haphazard yet imaginatively forceful allusions in a coherent framework of explanation. No doubt Freud himself, confronted with the speech, would go a step further, and claim a phallic reference in Leontes' curious allusion to his 'muzzled dagger' at 156. Any reader who thinks such a interpretation wildly unhistorical should consult *Richard III*, III. i. 110-23 (again an adult-child situation) before reaching his conclusion.

Hermione's 'Grace to boot!' has received attention from critics as well as commentators. It is often pointed out that this is one of several allusions to Grace made by Hermione, and that these allusions have the cumulative effect of investing Hermione with a sort of sanctity. This is perfectly true on one imaginative level. But it is worth noticing (particularly since it will bring us naturally to the last element in the Freudian account) that there is another level at which the words have an almost opposite effect. Apprehended as an image-pattern the allusions to Grace seem to hint something prelapsarian about Hermione, Eve confronted by the Serpent. Taken in their dialectic context, they are fundamentally postlapsarian. Hermione says 'Grace to boot!' when she feels herself under an imputation of sin. When at line 99 she says 'O, would her name were Grace!' the context is very similar. Leontes has complimented her on her persuading Polixenes to stay, and has suggested that she has spoken to better purpose only once. For some reason this throws her into confusion. Her exclamation shows that she fears his revelation will shame her in some way, and when she returns to the word, at line 105, it is to express relief.

If the reader can be induced to drop for a moment the stereotype of Hermione as Ideal Wifehood, he may be willing to follow out the last stage in the Freudian interpretation. Here it was suggested that while Leontes' attitude is unquestionably unbalanced it nevertheless retains a certain cognitive force; that there is some real sexual content in Hermione's behaviour to Polixenes, which Leontes' pathological vigilance has perceived and wildly inflated. There need be no suggestion that Hermione is anything but a good and faithful wife, in the ordinary meaning of those terms. But, as her language indicates, she is not an ideal woman, but a virtuous woman in a imperfect world. Such good women cannot but feel momentary impulses of sexual attraction towards men not their husbands, and these impulses are cushioned and absorbed by a convention of manners which prudently affords them a certain scope. There is no doubt of Hermione's essential fidelity to her husband. The question is: does she *flirt* with Polixenes?

It certainly looks as if she does, but we are confronted here by an historical difficulty. The fine discrimination of flirtatiousness from ordinary affectionate politeness requires, it may be, a closer knowledge of Jacobean manners than we in fact possess. C. S. Lewis has suggested[1] that before the eighteenth century manners were in general far more extravagant than they are today. If we were transported back to that time, we might at first have difficulty in distinguishing, say, a nobleman's natural aristocratic bearing from an upstart's strut. Likewise, we might mistake a great lady's natural effusiveness for an erotic advance. Obviously, these considerations suggest a *caveat* for anyone trying to assess the precise erotic tenor of this scene.

But, equally obviously, we must try. First of all, despite the fact that Shakespeare frequently treats of high-life, there is in his work no real parallel to this mannered and affectionate volubility, presented as it is in no spirit of parody. Secondly, there is a sense in which Shakespeare's writing of the scene undercuts historical speculation about manners. For there can be little doubt that in any case there is no point at which Hermione definitely transgresses against good taste. One is left saying, 'Well, such high manners would surely be likely to breed considerable suppressed erotic tension.' The fact that the erotic elements in this scene are latent rather than overt places our problem out of the reach of any sociological research.

It may be that the first hint of nervous tension is felt at line 42, where

[1] In his essay 'Addison', printed in *Eighteenth Century Essays*, ed. J. L. Clifford (New York, 1959), pp. 144-56.

Hermione, in a manner not wholly necessary, suddenly assures Leontes that in fact she loves him. She then begins her courtesy-wooing of Polixenes. We cannot judge this speech by comparing it with what a modern hostess would say. But we can certainly see a marked contrast between her warmth and assiduity and Leontes' coolness (though Leontes is presumably putting up a reasonably good show so far). Further, it is strange that she no sooner has her triumph (Polixenes will stay) than she begins her strange teasing of Polixenes on the subject of his and Leontes' childhood. Her tone can only be described as 'roguish'. And it appears to spring naturally from her exuberance at successfully wooing Polixenes to stay. That Polixenes senses an element of flirtation in her questioning is strongly implied by the suggestive gallantry with which he closes the exchange. I have said that in this speech he turns the tables on Hermione. But, in another way, the triumph is hers, since she has overcome his idealistic refusal to admit a sexual element into their conversation. Then come the allusions to Grace which, as has already been suggested, seem to betray some want of confidence, on Hermione's part, in the purity of her own soul. When Leontes rejoins Hermione and Polixenes he at once bends his efforts, in an almost childlike way, to the task of reminding Hermione of his own relation to her. He tries to draw her attention by comparing her new (social) triumph over Polixenes with her old triumph over *him*. There is something fleetingly desperate about Leontes' intrusion of his own love-affair with Hermione into the conversation. But he does not get the reassurance he craves. His efforts are—ever so slightly—snubbed by Hermione, who for a moment seems to weigh her husband and Polixenes in either hand, and then to turn to Polixenes.

> Why lo you now; I have spoke to th' purpose twice:
> The one, for ever earn'd a royal husband;
> Th' other, for some while a friend.
> > [*Giving her hand to Polixenes*] (I. ii. 106-8)

There is no stage-direction in the Folio. The one I have given is Capell's. But it is very probable. Certainly she turns away from Leontes, for his next speech is a soliloquy. Equally certainly, seven lines later she is holding Polixenes' hand, for this time the Folio text tells us so. This would be the natural point for her to take his hand.

It is odd how much material is given to the reader who would take this scene in a Freudian way. The psychoanalyst's sense of a latent ambiguity in the childhood love of Leontes and Polixenes,[1] in the sociable affection of Hermione, is, I think, really present in the play. Yet to stress this aspect is to falsify; or at least, to distort, since it transforms what is essentially background into foreground. In an age which is naturally drawn to the oblique, the difficult and the sour, it is hard to write of the foreground. But it is very important to do so, if only to reveal a fundamental difference between Freud and Shakespeare. Freud once wrote that he had never become a great surgeon or healer because he did not have that fundamental desire to hurt and maim which is compensated by the adoption of such altruistic professions.[2] It is easy to see that in propositions like this the categories of value have been emptied of all significance. In Shakespeare it is otherwise; it seems peculiarly characteristic of his genius to give the dark gods their head and yet retain the common values, to allow the submerged cross-currents to spend their strength and yet leave goodness valuable and love real. Without placing Shakespeare 'on the heights' for his final period (as Dowden did), one yet feels that there is something very sane and loving in his evident intuition that the presence of a half-conscious sexual element in Hermione's relation to Polixenes in no way *infects* her, that Leontes' boyhood love for Polixenes was as beautiful as it was perilous. For, ultimately, it is Hermione's loving chastity which is dominant in the scene, not her flirtatiousness. Polixenes' imagery of sunlight and timeless innocence sing louder in our ears than the counter-suggestions of childish misdemeanours. The metaphors of growth and freshness surrounding Mamillius are quite unimpaired. The imagery of natural decay and rebirth, of life coming out of death which began in the opening scene continues in this. Leontes describes his courtship of Hermione in terms of seasonal falling away followed by renewal (I. ii. 102-3) and the image he uses to express Hermione's yielding—'open thy white hand' suggests her purity with a power which is too strong for all the cross-currents I have noted. The dark background and the bright

[1] C.f. Northrop Frye, 'Recognition in *The Winter's Tale*', *Fables of Identity* (New York, 1963), pp. 113-14, '. . . a careful reader of the text may suspect that the references to his youth have touched off some kind of suppressed guilt.'

[2] See his 'Postscript' (1927) to *The Question of Lay Analysis*, in *The Complete Psychological Works of Sigmund Freud*, trans. J. Strachey (1959), vol. XX, p. 253.

foreground (excepting for the moment Leontes) are not at odds with one another. Rather, each imparts a kind of authority to the other. There is a sense in which Hermione in her full humanity (for so she is presented) is more lovable than Hermione the Ideal (whom the critics would foist upon us).

With Leontes there is of course no problem of confounding background and foreground. The dark gods have made him their own, have emerged into full view. Thus it is far less disturbing to see Leontes psychoanalysed than it is to see Hermione psychoanalysed. Also, Leontes is much simpler material for psychoanalysis. For example, it is quite easy to show that he has a divided mind. At II. i. 68 we have a perfect example of a Freudian slip, and a further confirmation of the theory of projected jealousy—

> Praise her but for this her without-door form
> (Which on my faith deserves high speech) and straight
> The shrug, the hum or ha, these petty brands
> That calumny doth use—O, I am out,
> That mercy does . . .

Part of his mind admits his calumny while the other part commits it.

But equivocation is not so much an occasional feature as a constant in Leontes' speeches. Sexual double-entendres come in such numbers that the conscientious annotator could fill pages with them. M. M. Mahood, in her book, *Shakespeare's Wordplay* (1957), distinguishes conscious from unconscious punning.[1] For example I. ii. 123-5 ('*neat*, not *neat*, but *cleanly*, captain:/ And yet the steer, the heifer and the calf/Are all called *neat*') must count as a conscious pun, even if Leontes is not fully aware of all the pressures which drive him to his beast-imagery. On the other hand at I. ii. 117-18 ('. . . and then to sigh, as 'twere/The mort o' th' deer') the choice of words may be dictated by a quite unconscious reference to the ambiguity present (for Jacobean ears) in the word 'deer', and even perhaps, to the unspoken word 'die' which may lie behind the passage. Perhaps the most intricate of Leontes' equivocations occurs at line 187—

> Go, play, boy, play: thy mother plays, and I
> Play too; but so disgrac'd a part, whose issue
> Will hiss me to my grave.

[1] p. 149.

Miss Mahood's analysis of this is so good that it must be quoted at length:

> Only the first *play* is used in a single sense. We might paraphrase Leontes' *double-entendres* thus: 'Go and amuse yourself; your mother is also pretending to play by acting the kind hostess, but I know that she is a real daughter of the game and up to another sport which makes me act the contemptible role of the deceived husband. So for the moment I'm playing her like a fish ("I am angling now") by giving her line.' This ironic wordplay of Leontes is sustained through *disgraced*, meaning both 'ungraceful' and 'shameful', and *issue* meaning 'exit', 'result' and perhaps also 'Polixenes' bastard child that Hermione now carries': But *play*, *disgraced* and *issue* have other functions besides that of rendering Leontes' paroxysm true to life. Shakespeare counters each of Leontes' puns by further meanings which relate the word to the larger context of the play's thought and action. The meaning 'make-believe' is added in this way to all the senses of *play*. Leontes is play-acting in his outburst; it is characteristic of such obsessions as his that the sufferer is deluded, yet half knows he is under a delusion —as when we know we are in a nightmare but cannot wake from it. Only the make-believe of Hermione, in playing at being a statue, and the make-believe of Perdita, in playing the part of a shepherd's daughter, can restore Leontes to a sane discrimination between illusion and reality.[1]

It is interesting, and not wholly irrelevant, to reflect how unlikely we are to come upon criticism of this kind before the time of Sigmund Freud. Freud seldom or never wrote anything true about a specific work of art, yet left to the twentieth century as a legacy a renewed sensitivity to poetic ambiguities.

Leontes' language will soon take the fat off a sensibility used to more sedentary material. It raises questions at every turn. Why, for example, are lines 112 and 117 hypermetrical? Is it a deliberate device of metrical synaesthesia, designed to convey the feel of passion breaking free from restraint? What, precisely, is the ambiguity of Leontes' question to Mamillius at line 127—'Art thou my calf?' Is it a combination of the sort of playful, half-meaningless appeal thrown out by all parents—'Are you Daddy's boy?' with the more frightening doubt—'Are you really my son?' It is not always easy to apply Miss Mahood's distinction

[1] *Op. cit.*, pp. 149-150.

between unconscious and conscious wordplay. Leontes' words to Hermione at line 174

> How thou lov'st us, show in our brother's welcome . . .

could be a private joke (of a bitter kind) between Leontes and himself, or the equivocation could have arisen through a quite involuntary crossing of lines in his head. The obscurity generated by this duality of mind can reach desperate proportions. Take lines 137-46

> Can thy dam?—may 't be?—
> Affection! thy intention stabs the centre:
> Thou dost make possible things not so held,
> Communicat'st with dreams;—how can this be?—
> With what's unreal thou coactive art,
> And fellow'st nothing: then 'tis very credent
> Thou may'st co-join with something; and thou dost,
> (And that beyond commission) and I find it,
> (And that to the infection of my brains
> And hard'ning of my brows).

Polixenes' comment ('What means Sicilia?') is, one feels, pardonable. First of all, 'thou' is best taken as referring to 'Affection' (not Mamillius). 'Affection' almost certainly means 'violent passion', as it does in Leonato's words to Claudio and Pedro, in *Much Ado About Nothing*:

> By my troth, my lord, I cannot tell what to think of it but that she loves him with an enraged affection . . . (II. iii. 105-7)

—or again in Mardian's words to Cleopatra:

> Yet I have fierce affections, and think
> What Venus did with Mars. (*Antony and Cleopatra*, I. v. 17)

A particularly interesting analogue occurs in a speech of Othello; interesting because Othello's speech, like Leontes', seems to be troubled by an element of obscure sexuality:

> I therefore beg it not
> To please the palate of my appetite,
> Nor to comply with heat,—the young affects
> In me defunct,—and proper satisfaction . . . (*Othello*, I. iii. 261-5)

'Affects' is here a noun, equivalent to 'affections'. 'Intention', in Leontes' speech, probably means 'intensity'. The king, drawing sanity from his child's clear eye, is at first objective. The Cambridge editor paraphrases thus: '. . . thou makest impossible things seem possible, partakest of the nature of dreams, cooperatest with unreality, and becomest fellow-worker with what does not exist.' Thus far his perception of the true state of affairs persists. Then, at line 142, madness reasserts itself. Suddenly (by a fallacious *a fortiori*) Leontes finds himself arguing that if the fantasies of passion can attach themselves to unrealities, how much *more* probable it is that they will attach themselves to realities. His neurosis works with a kind of sub-logical cunning. It may be significant that the revolution in his mind occurs at the word 'nothing'. There is a whole crescendo of 'nothings' in the frightening speech extending from line 284 to 296. Leontes seems to have intermittent intuitions of nihilism. One is reminded of Lear's terrified repetition of the same word as he stares over the edge into darkness in his encounter with Cordelia (*King Lear*, I. i. 88ff.).

The imprisonment of Leontes' mind is wonderfully conveyed by this system of ambiguities, which again and again refer us back to the delusion, away from the public and objective. The same self-imprisonment appears in his overt behaviour. In lines 273f. he specially constructs his interrogation of Camillo in such a way that *anything* Camillo does will 'confirm' his theory. But the *horror* of Leontes' condition is communicated in a series of repulsive images—beasts and fish at 123, 180 and 195 and the dreadful 'I have drunk and seen the spider' at II. i. 45, which can be read either as a metaphor of spiritual disease or as a literal description of the sort of hallucination that can spring *from* such a disease (analogous to the phenomena of *delirum tremens*). We may remember that Leontes himself brought a clinical terminology to bear on his condition in the first words which made it manifest—

I have *tremor cordis* on me (I. ii. 110)

If the foregoing examination of Act I Scene ii has achieved its purpose, it will have given some idea of the range and complexity of Shakespeare's craft in *The Winter's Tale*.

This scene is immensely complex and marvellously organised. It will doubtless be objected that my account is too subtle for theatrical practice; that it represents a 'study-reading'. Certainly, I could never claim that such critical language as I have been using would pass through a spectator's mind as he watched the play. But I would claim that his responses (so long has he was not brainwashed in advance by some simplistic interpretation) would be so complex as to require such terminology for their analysis. A truly exhaustive account of the reactions of an intelligent man watching the first act of *Hamlet* would fill a book many times the length of the present study. The sensibility of a man sitting in a theatre is not limited to such univocal responses as 'Oh how innocent!' or 'Oh how corrupt!' When Hermione reacts with a joyous confusion on being praised by her husband, the intelligent observer will see that her language is neither naïve nor faux-naïf but is rather the achieved innocence of a good woman in a fallen world. He may lack the language to say this at the time, but he may recognise the appropriateness of such language afterwards. And, if he is very wide-awake, he will notice an element of nervous fear in her speech. At this level of subtlety, however, I will admit that the audience is likely to divide itself into the aware and the unaware. The women, for example, are more likely to notice than the men. Incidentally, without such inequalities and un-illuminated areas in understanding, there would be no excuse at all for interpretative criticism. It seems a dubious exercise in critical economy to reject as 'untheatrical' everything which is revealed to us by a special effort of attention. The rest of the play's first half must be dealt with in a much more summary fashion.

Act II opens with the curious and touching episode of the pregnant Hermione joking with Mamillius and her ladies-in-waiting. The jesting takes the form (as often in Shakespeare) of a sort of sexual teasing between the adults and the child. It is curious that humour which turns on the startling precociousness of the child should nevertheless succeed in conveying an impression of innocence. The tranquillity is broken by the entry of Leontes. The poignancy of this loving conversation and its violent conclusion should be compared with the closely parallel scene in *Macbeth* (IV. ii) where Lady Macduff teases her son before they are cut down by the murderers. Leontes enters just as Mamillius is beginning his sad winter's tale about the man who lived by a churchyard. The man in the story ('of sprites and goblins') is suddenly replaced by a strangely similar man, attended by misshapen, ancient creatures of the mind. In a way, the effect is cinematic: a sudden, shocking close-up. We thought we were to be regaled with a tale of remote horrors, but instead we are confronted by them. Leontes finds the flight of Camillo and Polixenes evidence for his theory, as he finds *everything* evidence for his theory (compare I. ii. 273f. above, and II. iii. 11f. below). He begins (line 36, 'How blest am I . . .') to find a strange exhilaration in his degradation. His Freudian equivocations continue; e.g. at line 48 'All's true that is mistrusted' has the surface-meaning 'All my suspicions are well-founded', but will also bear the under-meaning 'All those whom I suspect are really loyal'. Leontes accuses Hermione of infidelity. Hermione is as amazed as any modern critic at the suddenness of Leontes' jealousy. But where we turn to psychology, she in order to fill up the vacuum in her knowledge draws on astronomical lore— 'There's some ill planet reigns' (105). As her crisis becomes clearer to her, she becomes more magnificent—

> Who is't that goes with me? Beseech your highness,
> My women may be with me, for you see
> My plight requires it. (116-18)

Her bearing has both regality and a moving, natural candour as she draws attention to her physical condition. Throughout this scene, her queenly authority contrasts with Leontes' petulant ranting—

Hermione.　　　My women, come; you have leave.
Leontes.　Go, do our bidding: hence! (124-5)

The next scene opens with Paulina at the prison gate. She is a quasi-comic character, and provides a lifting note of common personality. One is reminded of De Quincey's essay on the knocking at the door in *Macbeth*. Paulina curiously reverses the figure of the 'porter of hell-gate'. The Porter in *Macbeth* is essentially obstructive. Paulina is essentially aperient. If he is the Comic Immovable Object, she is the Comic Irresistible Force. Where the Porter is associated with venereal disease and sexual decay, Paulina is associated with fertility. She acts as midwife to that great birth of the last act to which Autolycus is pandar. Hermione, we learn, has been delivered of a child, 'lusty, and like to live' (27). The matter-of-fact phrase gives one a momentary insight into Jacobean infant-mortality. At the close of the scene her language takes on a profounder note—

> This child was prisoner to the womb, and is
> By law and process of great nature, thence
> Free'd and enfranchis'd . . . (59-61)

Nature stands behind Paulina. It (or she) works gloriously, independent of the neuroses of kings. Paulina promises her protection. For some reason we join Emilia in believing her, though she is only an eccentric humorist in a woman's world.

The scene changes to Leontes' palace. The king is discovered, raving. After some lines of soliloquy and conversation with a servant (on the subject of Mamillius, who has 'languished'), Paulina bursts in. There is a short tussle at the door but entry-forcing is Paulina's *forte*. But her trump card, the baby, fails of its desired effect. Leontes is not won over. Instead he seizes the child and instructs Antigonus to kill it. Paulina's mission is disastrous. Anyone who does not know the rest of the play will feel the trust we all put forth at the end of the last scene to have been misplaced. Yet even in the scene of her defeat her speech again takes on its note of liturgical power (at line 114 she calls Leontes a 'heretic'), again evokes the image of nature, now explictly deified. The sentence in which the image occurs is also notable for a strange paralogism on Paulina's part:

> And thou, good goddess Nature, which hast made it
> So like to him that got it, if thou hast
> The ordering of the mind too, 'mongst all colours
> No yellow in't, lest she suspect, as he does,
> Her children not her husband's! (II. iii. 103-7)

This is illogical because of the asymmetry of the biological process. Since Perdita (the child) is female, she could never, however jealous she was, suspect that her children were not really hers. It would be pleasant to think that this is delicate comedy, catching very accurately the sort of confusion an excited woman might easily commit. The Arden editor thinks so, and he has a parallel from Thackeray. If it is (and it is certainly entirely in character) the demands it makes on the wits of the audience are steep indeed.

At the end of Act II Hermione's state is low. She is rejected by her husband. Her new-born child she has staked and lost. We do not see her in her grief, but learn a little of the shock she sustained later, at III. ii. 98-101. Act III opens with a sudden, but brief, change of atmosphere —Cleomenes and Dion on the holy island of Delphos. The opening words are especially haunting—

> The climate's delicate, the air most sweet,
> Fertile the isle, the temple much surpassing
> The common praise it bears.

These lines refer both backwards and forwards in Shakespeare's œuvre. The reference back, as we have learned to expect, is to *Macbeth*:

Duncan. This castle hath a pleasant seat: the air
Nimbly and sweetly recommends itself
Unto our gentle senses.
Banquo. This guest of summer,
The temple-haunting martlet, does approve
By his lov'd mansionry that the heaven's breath
Smells wooingly here: no jutty, frieze,
Buttress, nor coign of vantage, but this bird
Hath made his pendant bed and procreant cradle:
Where they most breed and haunt, I have observ'd
The air is delicate. (I. vi. 1-10)

The passage, like its fellow in *The Winter's Tale* has the force of fresh air, breathed deeply after an experience of claustrophobia. The theme of birth and renewal, implicit in *The Winter's Tale* version, is here explicit. But, as before, the later play turns the passage inside out. Duncan was tragically wrong about the life-giving properties of Macbeth's castle. But Cleomenes and Dion move in a divine comedy. They are, against all expectation, right to experience joy. The forward reference is to *The Tempest*. I give the passage with some omissions:

Adrian. Though this is land seem to be desert, uninhabitable,
and almost inaccessible, yet it must needs be of
subtle, tender, and delicate temperance. The air
breathes upon us here most sweetly.
Sebastian. As if it had lungs, and rotten ones.
Antonio. Or as 'twere perfumed by a fen.
Gonzalo. Here is everything advantageous to life.
How lush and lusty the grass looks! how green!
Antonio. The ground indeed is tawny.
Sebastian. With an eye of green in 't. (II. i. 35-55)

Again we have the key words 'delicate', 'air', 'sweet', again the context of renewed life. But, in the ambiguous isle of *The Tempest* the joyful perceptions of the good characters are countered by the sour perceptions of the bad. The audience itself never learns who is right and who wrong. In a way, each rewriting reflects the character of the play in which it appears; *Macbeth* tragic, *The Winter's Tale* happy, *The Tempest* ambiguous, the intimations of Paradise undercut by a doubt about reality.

We have barely filled our lungs with the air of Delphos before the stage, so to speak, darkens again for the trial scene. Leontes opens the proceedings with a somewhat oily speech in style reminiscent of Claudius' conciliatory speech in *Hamlet* (I. ii. 1-39). His appeal at line 4—

> Let us be clear'd
> Of being tyrannous, since we so openly
> Proceed in justice—

may seem to have a certain substance. Hermione contradicts him at line 31, and the Oracle at line 133, but he is finally refuted pragmatically, at line 140, when his attempt to disregard the Oracle proves him incapable of objectivity.

Some parts of Hermione's speeches in her own defence may have suffered somewhat from the progress of civilisation; in particular her profession of a high aristocratic stoicism, as at line 43:

> For life, I prize it
> As I weigh grief (which I would spare) . . .

We no longer extend an automatic admiration to anyone who is contemptuous of life. But I suspect that our unease is not purely the product of history. Hermione is too close to the Nature of the play to speak slightingly of life. But all this is redeemed by the quite different sublimity of

> Sir,
> You speak a language that I understand not:
> My life stands in the level of your dreams,
> Which I'll lay down. (79-82)

Here too she offers to give up life, but the speech is animated not so much by contempt of life as by a just estimation of its richness. Also we feel that her willingness to surrender her life has something to do with her love of Leontes. This moral advance colours (and improves) her return to the Stoic theme at lines 92 to 96. Now her words are ultimately consonant with the logic of the play as a whole, which demands that Hermione be in the end, not a despiser of life but a life-giver. She is not answered until IV. iv. 130, where Perdita, in response to Florizel's question, 'What, like a corpse?' cries, 'No, like a bank, for love to lie and play on.'

The Oracle's message is in Shakespeare's Laconic style, deemed suitable to antique material. Its manner is anticipated by Artemidorus's letter in *Julius Caesar* (II. iii. 1-8) and parodied by Falstaff (*2 Henry IV*, II, ii. 125-31). It vindicates Hermione. It is time for Leontes to repent and find himself again. But his salvation comes not from a supernatural but from a natural source. He resists the Oracle, but his heart is pierced by the news of the death of Mamillius immediately following. Paulina is given the marvellous drab words

> look down
> And see what death is doing (148-9)

as Hermione falls. Leontes' speech of repentance follows, and Paulina's ferocious castigation. It would seem that we must either find Paulina's behaviour grotesquely unnecessary or else find something as yet thin and only half-convincing in Leontes' breast-beating. I think the second alternative is the right one. The king's proposal to 'new-woo my queen, recall the good Camillo' (156) has too facile a confidence. Nevertheless there is something unpalatable in Paulina's disingenuous rhetorical understatement at lines 187 to 189, and something downright frightening in her sketch of possible penances for Leontes (210-13), though she relents a little at line 218. She is a goblin-figure, a little larger than life. Her ways and speech have something monstrous about them, alternately alarming and somehow enormously good.

Paulina's catalogue of Leontes' crimes suggests that all his sins were nothing to the sins against Hermione. In Shakespeare's principal source, Greene's *Pandosto*, the Hermione-figure really dies, and the great reconciliation is between the father and his daughter. Shakespeare's most important modification of his material is the sparing of Hermione for the final joining in love and forgiveness. He evidently felt, and makes us feel, that the relation between the husband and his wife is the really huge thing. Paulina dins it in our ears.

We are near the turning-point of the play. With scene iii of Act III the spatial reference of the play is suddenly extended. Hitherto, except for a brief glimpse of Delphos, we have been confined to Sicilia. Now we are transported to the desert coasts of Bohemia, and a storm is blowing up. The Mariner, by a commonplace trope, associates the tempest with Divine anger. Antigonus gives the notion a more mysterious ring by the late-plays language of his reply:

Their sacred wills be done! (7)

Left alone by the Mariner, Antigonus describes his vision of the ghost of Hermione, and then sets down the baby Perdita. The storm grows yet more violent and there follows the most celebrated stage-direction in Shakespeare, '*Exit, pursued by a bear.*' This is sometimes described as a crude device to get Antigonus off the stage at all costs. But that can hardly be the case, since he was about to leave anyway. We have been warned at line 12 that the place is famous for its wild beasts. It is likely that emergence of the bear is to be seen as part of the violent unleashing of the irrational forces of nature simultaneously at work in the Heavens. Yet I suspect that our impulse to laugh is foreseen and authorised by Shakespeare. The episode is frightening and funny at the same time; it is *eldritch*. Nature is terrible now, but in a way she is jovial. The comedians (Shepherd and Clown) are about to enter, in the midst of death and tempest. A sound of joy is almost audible in the wind as we are brought to the pivot of the play—

Shepherd. Now bless thyself: thou met'st with things dying, I with things new-born.

3. Bohemia: Varieties of Innocence

Now bless thyself: thou met'st with things dying, I with things new-born. (III. iii. 112-13)

We knew in a way before the Shepherd said this that the great counter-movement of the play had begun, but the words make our knowledge explicit. The storm is still raging, or else just beginning to fade. But the tempest which wrecked the ship and drowned her crew, like the bear who ate Antigonus, came over to us with a sort of irresponsible gaiety. Though *The Winter's Tale* is one of the Romances, and deals with the restoration of the apparently dead, it is not without its genuine casualties. But the Clown's description of them is summary, even sportive:

> But to make an end of the ship, to see how the sea flap-dragoned it: but first, how the poor souls roared, and the sea mocked them: and how the poor gentleman roared, and the bear mocked him, both roaring louder than the sea or weather . . . I have not winked since I saw these sights: the men are not yet cold under water, not the bear half dined on the gentleman: he's at it now. (III. iii. 97-105)

The Arden editor compares the description of the storm with Miranda's (*The Tempest*, I. ii. 2-13). As regards dramatic tone, a closer comparison might be Guiderius's jubilant account of his murder of Cloten in *Cymbeline* (IV. ii. 184f.). It is arguable that the tone is 'tasteless', in one sense of the word. But, in another, the taste is very sure. The touch is wonderfully light; take the Shepherd's unconscious self-revelation in his opening words (my italics):

> I would there were no age between ten and three-and-twenty, or that youth would sleep out the rest; for there is nothing in the between but getting wenches with child, *wronging the ancientry*, stealing, fighting . . . . (59-63)

It is plain that, *pace* Lytton Strachey, Shakespeare's interest in common humanity is as vigilant as ever. There is no dropping of a shutter between the great tragedies and the Romances. Indeed, the nearest analogue I know to the humour of this passage occurs in *Hamlet* (II. ii. 549), where the Prince is handing the players over to Polonius's care and adds (though the player he is addressing is apparently quite docile) 'follow that lord; and look you mock him not'. Hamlet, of course, is not joking. With both Hamlet and the Shepherd, the words are funny because they are unconsciously informative. But though the humour may be irresponsible towards the dead, it is responsible towards the living. It numbs our awareness of the shipwreck, but somehow sharpens our awareness of the baby, as for example at line 75, '. . . they were warmer that got this than the poor thing is here.'

However we may fret at the unaccustomed air, the thing has happened. We are in Bohemia now. Our spirits have been made to labour with the complexities of guilt and jealousy. Now they are to undertake another kind of work, as they are shown the equal complexities of innocence. If the pastoral world of Bohemia has something visionary about it, we should remember that it is a vision in the sense defined by William Blake:

> A Spirit and a Vision are not, as the modern philosophy supposes, a cloudy vapour, or a nothing; they are organized and minutely articulated beyond all that the mortal and perishing nature can produce.[1]

Babies take years to grow up, and plays take only hours to perform. So Shakespeare at this point in his story simply skips sixteen years. He does it with the help of a chorus, who is Time himself. Some readers are embarrassed by what they suppose to be the crudity of this device. Dramas, they feel (especially if they happen to have been brought up on Aristotle's *Poetics*), should not have so ostentatiously dual a structure. Such readers will normally prefer the construction of *The Tempest*, which observes the neo-classical Unities and handles all material prior to the reunion in long, narrative speeches. It is probably true that *The Tempest* has a certain abstract shapeliness and celerity which *The Winter's Tale* lacks. But it is, from one point of view, an expensive symmetry. Its unified plot has emptied *The Tempest* of any vivid sense of the difference between age and youth, winter and summer, loss and restoration.

Shakespeare's Time chorus is an unashamedly allegorical figure who has stepped out of an altogether older type of drama, perhaps with some assistance from the fashionable world of the Masque. If we remind ourselves that part of the special pleasure of masques consisted in recognising

[1] 'A Descriptive Catalogue' in *Poetry and Prose of William Blake*, ed. Geoffrey Keynes, 1956.

one's old friend X in the guise of Y, we may be tempted to an un-verifiable conjecture concerning the present chorus. At line 21 he says

> . . . remember well
> I mentioned a son o' th' king's . . .

But Time has not been on stage before. Might this have been an 'in-joke' for those in the audience who recognised that Shakespeare himself was playing the part of Time?

There follows a brief, 'functional' scene between Camillo and Polixenes in which a certain amount of information is filled in, and then we are introduced to Autolycus. It is hard to know how much significance we should attach to his name. The commentaries tell us that Shakespeare may have drawn the name either from Plutarch or (more probably) from the description in Golding's translation of Ovid's *Metamorphoses* of the wily thief 'Autolychús'. It is just possible that Shakespeare had access to the manuscript of Chapman's translation of the *Odyssey* which includes a description of a witty equivocator called Autolycus. The translation was not published till 1616, but there is good precedent for suggesting that Shakespeare read it before publication. Strachey's *True Reportory of the Wrack* was first published in *Purchas his Pilgrimes* (1625), but Shakespeare drew on it for *The Tempest*.

But the important thing is not so much Where did the name 'Auto-lycus' come from? as What did it bring with it? A sense of etymology gives us 'very wolf' or 'self-wolf'. The suggestion of voracity makes good sense.

Autolycus enters singing. The strange, pungent nature-poetry of his songs (like that of the great nature-hymn in the masque within *The Tempest*) has not, to my knowledge, been adequately described. Lines which could come from any Elizabethan song-book, such as

> Why then comes in the sweet o' the year

or

> For a quart of ale is a dish for a king

are fused with stranger, fiercer lines, like

> For the red blood reigns in the winter's pale

or the really marvellous image of sharp *awareness*

> Doth set my pugging tooth an edge.

We soon see Autolycus in his professional capacity gulling the Clown. But Autolycus, with all his cunning, is as free from real *sophistication* as his victims. His first song sets a tone which never needs to be modified —cunning, out-door weather, joy and rapacity. Autolycus is as innocent as a magpie or a kite. That is to say, he is utterly innocent, and utterly dishonest. His type of innocence, if squarely regarded (and Shakespeare is not a writer to blur these things) is not amenable to sentimental treatment.

The Clown's character is well sustained. Note that his sober line

Alas, poor man! a million of beating may come to a great matter

is addressed to an audience who know him already in his character of mathematician from his speech beginning at line 36 above.

And then Autolycus departs, as he came, singing. The scene serves both as an introduction to Autolycus and as a sort of prelude to the great pastoral which is to follow. As at the beginning of the play the courtiers preceded the kings, so here the lesser, pastoral figures go before the greater.

Thus, when Perdita and Florizel enter we are admitted to an imaginative experience which is the opposite of parody. Instead of seeing the heroic reduced by the mock-heroic, we see the familiar shabby rural world suddenly brighten into something larger and more beautiful. Autolycus spoke of Mercury (IV. iii. 25), the most slippery of the Olympians. Perdita and Florizel speak of Flora, Jupiter, Neptune and Apollo:

> The gods themselves,
> Humbling their deities to love, have taken
> The shapes of beasts upon them: Jupiter
> Became a bull, and bellow'd; the green Neptune
> A ram, and bleated; and the fire-rob'd god,
> Golden Apollo, a poor humble swain,
> As I seem now. (IV. iv. 25-30)

The power unleashed in these lines is immense. In some ways their Mediterranean splendour recalls *Antony and Cleopatra*, but really they come to us from a world at once more ancient and more intimate than anything in that play. *Antony and Cleopatra* is a Roman play. In these lines Greek myth recovers momentarily its pristine force. They celebrate sexuality, and tell of the transformations of the ancient gods, monstrous or absurd, impelled by love. Yet such an account of them may involve a certain error of perspective. If so, it is best cured by comparing a passage from Marlowe's *Hero and Leander*:[1]

> There might you see the gods in sundrie shapes,
> Committing headdie ryots, incest, rapes:
> For know, that underneath this radiant floure
> Was *Danaes* statue in a brazen tower,
> *Jove* slylie stealing from his sisters bed,
> To dallie with *Idalian Ganimed*,
> And for his love *Europa* bellowing loud,
> And tumbling with the rainbow in a cloud . . .

This fusion of jubilation and magnificence carries the passage into a region in which the categories of heroic or mock-heroic no longer apply. Yet I find in it little sense of the divine. Shakespeare's gods on the other hand have as much animal vigour as Marlowe's, yet their vigour coexists with a strange gravity, which teaches us that the things we are hearing of are, in a quite un-Christian way, holy.

But here we need a second, corrective comparison. At line 116 Perdita says

> O Proserpina,
> For the flowers now that, frighted, thou let'st fall
> From Dis's wagon!

Contrast with this the lines of Milton which haunted Keats:

> Not that fair field
> Of *Enna*, where Proserpin gath'ring flours
> Herself a fairer Floure by gloomy *Dis*
> Was gatherd, which cost *Ceres* all that pain
> To seek her through the world. (*Paradise Lost*, IV. 268-72)

The purpose of these comparisons is not to show Shakespeare's superiority as a poet. All the passages are great poetry; indeed great poetry is needed for the task in hand, which is to show, without any obtrusion for the moment of questions of sheer merit, the peculiar precision of Shakespeare's tone. We are now in a position to see that although Shakespeare imparts a gravity to his mythical figures, he somehow does it without

[1] I. 143-50, in *The Works of Christopher Marlowe*, ed. C. F. Tucker Brooke, 1910, p. 495.

any Miltonic remoteness. Milton's classical allusions are windows opening on a world which, while very beautiful, is inexpressibly distant. But Shakespeare's imagination is genuine classic to Milton's romantic. Despite the fact that the immediate sense of Perdita's lines is an expression of regret, the gods she speaks of are seen in full daylight. They have not the superadded beauty which hangs round lost Arcadias. They are what they are.

But this is not to deny that they are also part of a larger imaginative scheme. It is not an accident that, as decay gives place to resurgence, we should be reminded of the myth of Proserpine. And because Proserpine is the spring, the speech is full of flowers. One hesitates to analyse such poetry as this, I suppose because of a fear of violating something infinitely fragile. But the presentiment is false. Poetry as great as this is not fragile, but very strong. Perdita's speech is concerned, as the whole scene is, with life and marriage. She begins with the myth, passes through imagery of virginity to the fruition of 'bright Phoebus in his strength'.

Florizel too (unlike his corresponding figure in *The Tempest*, Ferdinand) is given wonderful lines; for example:

> What you do,
> Still betters what is done. When you speak, sweet,
> I'd have you do it ever: when you sing,
> I'd have you buy and sell so, so give alms,
> Pray so, and, for the ord'ring your affairs,
> To sing them too: when you do dance, I wish you
> A wave o' th' sea, that you might ever do
> Nothing but that, move still, still so,
> And own no other function. Each your doing,
> So singular in each particular,
> Crowns what you are doing in the present deeds,
> That all your acts are queens. (IV. iv. 135-46)

This passage is like Keats' *Ode to a Grecian Urn*, like parts of *Four Quartets*, like much of the poetry of Yeats, in that it is filled with a fascination with movement, but with movement held in the stillness of the contemplating imagination. Everything Perdita does instantaneously fills Florizel's consciousness, absorbs all his attention, excludes all other rivals. Thus everything she does is, *per impossibile*, superlative. The image of the wave, which preserves its form even while it is alive with movement, unites intellectual precision with imaginative power. Also, the movement of the wave is reflected in the movement of the verse, frequently chiastic (ABBA):

> . . . sell so, so give alms . . .
> . . . move still, still so . . .

As with Perdita's speech we find that minute particularity of detail is reflected in the larger design of the play. *The Winter's Tale* itself has a movement like that of water, at first ebbing, then refluent. The to-and-fro sequence appears elsewhere in the verse of the play, frequently at crucial moments:

> . . . thou met'st with things dying, I with things new-born (III. iii. 112-13)

Florizel.   What, like a corpse?
Perdita. No, like a bank for love to lie and play on (IV. iv. 129-30),

> . . . o'er and o'er divides him
> 'Twixt his unkindness and his kindness; th' one
> He chides to hell, and bids the other grow . . . (IV. iv. 552-4)

Perdita's response to Florizel's speech is extremely interesting. She says that had he not been a simple shepherd she would have feared that his wooing was false. In an indirect fashion this is a remark about rhetoric. Rhetoric, classically defined as the art of persuasion, has always been liable to a sort of self-consumption. If we ask ourselves why it is that that the great rhetoricians, Demosthenes, Cicero, Burke, never in fact *persuade* us of anything at all, we shall soon see that it is because they are, so obviously, orators. We distrust that which has a palpable design upon us. To recognise the arts of persuasion is to be proof against them. Hence arises anti-rhetorical rhetoric: speech which hopes to persuade by being so obviously unpersuasive. But it is a pity that a great poet should be limited by such expedients. Shakespeare has here eluded the problem altogether. Florizel, we know, means what he says. But were he an artful rhetorician of the court, Perdita could not help but doubt him. As it is, his pastoral pretence has lifted him out of the self-consuming prison of rhetoric into the possibility of truthfulness. Throughout the scene, playing-acting is a means of revelation, not of concealment.

Into the Pastoral world come the anti-pastoral figures of Polixenes and Camillo. They are welcomed but not assimilated by the festive society. Instead, they stand like stocks. After a while, Polixenes gets involved in a philosophical argument with Perdita (80-103). Perdita says that she does not like to plant gillyvors because they are the product of an artificial, horticultural process. Polixenes counters by saying that just as flowers are a natural phenomenon, so is horticulture a natural phenomenon; in just the same way, it is natural and right that the scion of a noble race should be married to a baser stock. Perdita argees. Polixenes then reverts to the point of departure; very well then, let her plant gillyvors. At this Perdita's spirit of opposition suddenly revives; she would no more plant a gillyvor in her garden than she would wish that Florizel courted her solely on account of her cosmetic attractions.

There is an evident inconsistency between Polixenes' theoretic recommendation of mixed breeding, and his real purpose in attending the festival, which is to save his son from an unworthy marriage. We thus have two Polixenes, the Polixenes of the philosophical argument, who is all for mixing up stocks, and the Polixenes of the story proper, who is all for aristocratic exclusiveness. The modern reader, forced to choose which is right, tends to side with the Polixenes of the argument. But if we remember that Perdita is in fact not base at all but the daughter of Leontes (which means that the match is instinctively 'proper') we may be willing to consider the less palatable alternative. That is, we may try to think of Polixenes as a misguided sophister in argument, but as behaving like a good parent and guardian when practical matters hit him. This reading has the advantage of placing Perdita on the 'right' side in the dispute. After all the happy ending of the play marries noble stock to noble stock.

Some readers may feel that such a reading is ruled out by the fact that Polixenes' *arguments* are so much better than Perdita's. If Polixenes outmanœuvres Perdita then of course, it might be said, his case must be the right one and hers the wrong. I think it must be granted that Polixenes' arguments are better than Perdita's, since she can hardly be said to have arguments at all. But that Polixenes' position is philosophically the stronger is very questionable. By calling everything 'natural' he has effectually emptied the word of any content. When Perdita rallies, and produces a paradigm case (cosmetics as opposed to natural loveable-ness) she is working like a good linguistic philosopher; that is to say, she is exhibiting the word 'natural' as it is in ordinary action, where it does a perfectly legitimate job of distinguishing. Polixenes' use of 'natural' would certainly have been stigmatised by the late J. L. Austin as 'philo-

sophers' language'. Perdita's reply can easily be translated into argu-
mentative form: 'You say there's no distinction between art and nature.
But surely there is a perfectly clear distinction between e.g. falling in
love with a girl for her natural beauty and goodness on the one hand
and falling in love with a piece of artful cosmetic-work on the other.
The expression of this distinction is one of the functions of our art/nature
terminology.'

The real disadvantage of the second reading is that it is morally
offensive. Obviously if one has an *a priori* conviction that Shakespeare
can do nothing wrong, one will be compelled, analytically, to adopt
the first reading. I am myself inclined to the view that the second reading
is the right one, and that it *is* offensive. The egalitarian world of the
pastoral could never be more than an interlude for Shakespeare. The
court with its hierarchy was always the profounder, harder reality.
Duke Senior in the Forest of Arden is effusive on the merits of the simple
life, but at the end of the play there is no question but that he should go
back to his dukedom. When Perdita says

> The selfsame sun that shines upon his court
> Hides not his visage from our cottage, but
> Looks on alike (IV. iv. 445-7)

she is backed by scriptural authority, yet her assertion retains the status
of a pretty fancy only. She is mocked by her own unconscious aristo-
cracy. I cannot pretend that I like this, but I believe it is there, in the
text. Some may be comforted by telling themselves that Shakespeare
is writing for men to whom the social hierarchy is not an arbitrary
imposition, but something authorised by nature. But while the filial
and marital relationships treated in the Romances retain this authority,
the ideal of 'breeding' now stands in need of elaborate historicist defence.

I have described Autolycus as 'innocent'. I must now apply the same
word (for it is relevant) to a very different character, Perdita. Perhaps
the best way to describe the innocence of Perdita is to compare her with
the young women in *Love's Labour's Lost*. The girls in the earlier play
are smart, diamond-hard coquettes; they 'play hard to get', they are
engaged in a kind of erotic war with the young men and in this war,
because where the young men are soft and overtly emotional they are
the cold mistresses of their wits, they repeatedly triumph. In some ways
they resemble the girls in certain American films of the '30s. I once

heard a man remark that when these films were made all men must have been conversational masochists. The ferocity of these young women is explicable in social terms. Their behaviour presupposes a society in which women are inferior. Hence their rudest remarks have a quality of 'cheek' even before they begin to be witty. In the same way a remark made by a schoolboy to a master might be cruelly funny, yet the same remark made by one master to another in the Common Room be merely offensive.

But 'cheek' is not appropriate to a queen. Perdita, masquerading as queen of the festival, reveals her genuine royalty. Only real queens know how to abdicate. In her moment of seeming defeat her language recalls Cleopatra's. Here is Perdita:

> . . . I'll queen it no inch farther,
> But milk my ewes, and weep. (IV. iv. 450-1)

And here Cleopatra:

> No more, but e'en a woman, and commanded
> By such poor passion as the maid that milks.
> (*Antony and Cleopatra*, IV. xiii. 73-4)

Perdita is without hypocrisy, above the tactical triumphs of the bright young things in *Love's Labour's Lost*. She speaks with the sweet candour of the late-Shakespearean heroine. It is impossible to imagine Rosaline, Maria or Katherine saying to their attendants

> . . . yours,
> That wear upon your virgin branches yet
> Your maidenheads growing (IV. iv. 114-16)

or of their lovers (in their presence)

> No more than, were I painted, I would wish
> This youth should say 'twere well, and only therefore
> Desire to breed by me.

Perdita loves with a directness—one might almost say an objectivity— which is far more frightening than the caustic flirtation of a Rosaline, and far more attractive. In *Love's Labour's Lost* the man in black prevails over the lovers in the sombre truce which ends the play. The young are educated by the old. But the winter figures of the later play, Polixenes and Camillo, encounter lovers who are stronger than they. The old are educated by the young.

Perdita is innocent, then, in the directness of her love. But, in other respects it is evident that her innocence, like Hermione's, unlike Autolycus's, is an achieved innocence. It is the fruit of high intelligence and consideration, the flower rather than the root of her personality. Thus there are moments when her sophistication is so complete that one is tempted to say that she is the very opposite of innocent. Take, for example, her wonderfully adept speech of maidenly modesty at line 583:

> Your pardon, sir; for this
> I'll blush you thanks.

Yet after all it is not incompatible with innocence; for the maidenly modesty is quite real. Her high social skill has, paradoxically, lifted her into a region where she can tell the truth, just as the play-acting of the Pastoral revealed more than it disguised. Boorishness is not the same thing as innocence. Perdita actually refers to the liberating properties of their disguises in lines which have exactly the same quality of achieved innocence:

> . . . but that our fests
> In every mess have folly, and the feeders
> Digest it with a custom, I should blush
> To see you so attir'd; swoon, I think,
> To show myself a glass. (IV. iv. 10-14)

That Perdita is more cultivated than the country people among whom she lives is gently asserted at several points in the play. In Act IV, scene iii, the Clown is clearly bewildered by the elaborate shopping-list given him by Perdita. At IV. iv. 55 the old shepherd draws a contrast between the sort of simple, tipsy hospitality extended by his wife in the old days and Perdita's more aloof bearing. Evidently, Perdita is not to be taken as a simple instance of old-style rural housekeeping.

Perdita and Autolycus represent the extreme varieties of innocence. It is possible to argue that Autolycus's is the profounder sort. There is a brilliant short story by Graham Greene[1] about a man who returns to the town where as a child of seven he experienced a great love for a little girl living in the neighbourhood; he remembers how he wrote a message,

[1] 'The Innocent', printed in his *Twenty-one Stories* (Uniform Edition, 1954), pp. 51-6.

explaining his love, and left it for the girl to find in a certain hiding place. He recalls how he went again and again to the hiding-place, but she had not taken it away. Wondering what he wrote, he finds his way to the old spot. The paper is still there. He takes it out, and finds that it is a crudely obscene drawing. In summary the story must sound like a cynical attack on innocence. In fact it is not. The narrator of the story is only momentarily shocked. He then begins to wonder if the drawing were not made in all innocence as the direct expression of a fundamentally sexual attitude, whether innocence may not produce the same phenomenon as vulgarity.

The story is more favourable to Autolycus than to Perdita. There is certainly a sense in which the primal innocence of Autolycus is nowhere so apparent as in his almost continuous, pre-moral indecency. Doubtless, in any production of the play which suffered from a weak Perdita, there would be a danger that Autolycus's unreflecting impropriety would make Perdita's modesty seem deviously self-conscious, that the audience would see in Autolycus the *real* pastoral, and in Perdita only a consummately civilised imitation.

But such a production would be a falsification of the play. We may take first Autolycus's unblinking account of the monstrous examples of parturition and of frigidity retailed in his ballads:

> Here's one, to a very doleful tune, how a usurer's wife was brought to bed of twenty money-bags at a burden, and how she longed to eat adders' heads and toads carbonadoed . . . it was thought she was a woman, and was turned into a cold fish for she would not exchange flesh with one that loved her. (IV. iv. 263-82)

Autolycus is innocent in this passage by virtue of his evident independence of any moral system. The lines express neither approbation nor blame, only a sort of routine astonishment. Yet is would plainly be absurd to hold Autolycus *responsible* for his uncensorious attitude. The speech contributes to the imaginative celebration of fruitfulness which runs through the entire scene and is ritually enacted in dance by the 'twelve satyrs' at line 344. Let us now turn to one of Perdita's contributions to that celebration:

> I would I had some flowers o' th' spring, that might
> Become your time of day; and yours, and yours,
> That wear upon your virgin branches yet

> Your maidenheads growing . . .
>   . . . daffodils,
> That come before the swallow dares, and take
> The winds of March with beauty; violets, dim,
> But sweeter than the lids of Juno's eyes
> Or Cytherea's breath; pale primroses,
> That die unmarried, ere they can behold
> Bright Phoebus in his strength (a malady
> Most incident to maids) (IV. iv. 113-25)

The innocence of this speech is not pre-moral, but it is guiltless. Perdita's eye is as clear as Autolycus's, her language as unflinching. Her modesty is evidently not to be confused with a vulgar prudery. Her words are undoubtedly highly civilised, but there seems to be a point at which civilisation, if taken far enough, conducts us to a fresh possibility of simplicity. The uncivilised man (or the unsocialised man) may speak like Autolycus; the almost civilised girl will speak like Rosaline or Katherine. The fully civilised woman will speak like Perdita.

I have said that the innocence of Autolycus is not amenable to senti-mental treatment; that is to say, it cannot be adequately acted or described in sentimental terms. Yet *to prefer Autolycus to Perdita* may indeed be a peculiarly modern form of sentimentalism. The truth is that Autolycus's innocence is the sort that causes objective harm, Perdita's objective good.

D

4. Conclusion

Act V brings us back to Leontes. It is evident from the first words of the act that his sixteen years of penance have been performed in faithful sincerity. He does not suspect that Hermione is still alive. It is a convention of Elizabethan dramaturgy that one character may subject another to the most extreme mental cruelty and then make all well again simply by saying, 'I did this but to try thee.' For example, Act IV scene iii of *Mabeth* opens with a dialogue between Malcolm, the rightful heir to the throne of Scotland, and the nobleman Macduff. Malcolm deliberately strains the loyalty of Macduff past breaking point by pretending that if he obtained the crown his reign would be even more vicious than that of the usurping Macbeth. Once Macduff has been driven by despair to lament his country's fate, to dedicate himself to exile and to revile his once believed sovereign, then, and only then, does Malcolm permit himself a change of expression:

> Macduff, this noble passion,
> Child of integrity, hath from my soul
> Wip'd the black scruples, reconcil'd my thoughts
> To thy good truth and honour. (IV. iii. 114-17)

At first sight, Paulina's voluntary silence on the fact that Hermione is alive must appear one of the most extreme instances extant of the 'I-did-this-but-to-try-thee' complex. But it is not a pure instance. According to the normal use of the convention, the possibility that the very act of testing may have a psychological effect on the person tested is not admitted. The period of trial simply yields reassuring information. But Paulina actually *wishes* to affect Leontes. It is part of her design that his long period of trial should affect him spiritually. It is as if the playwright had at first satisfied our demand for realism by allowing that an arduous test affects the patient, but had thereupon shocked us by suggesting that the result would be not deleterious but beneficial. It is interesting that the modern view that it is 'morbid' to dwell on past misdoings is twice assumed in the play; by Cleomenes at V. i. 20f., and by Camillo at V. iii. 49f. Cleomenes is sharply reproved by Paulina, and Camillo, one presumes, escapes only because Paulina has more important business on hand. The need for a penance is partially accounted for by Leontes' obviously inadequate expression of regret at III. ii. 153f., but the sequestration of Hermione through all those years is a thing which neither priest nor psychiatrist would normally take upon himself to suggest. It is sometimes said that the oddity of Paulina's behaviour would never be noticed in actual theatrical performance. I think it more probable that we are meant to gasp, to find something non-natural, even monstrous in it. Paulina's character was not shaped in a human mould. That her restoration of Hermione coincides with the return of Perdita is not, we feel, due to mere psychological opportunism on her part. It rather suggests that she has access to a profounder source of authority.

Florizel, arriving, is parallelled in our minds with Mamillius (V. i. 115-18). The seasonal imagery is heard again, like music, at V. i. 150:

> Welcome hither,
> As is the spring to th' earth.

Some seventy lines later we come to the only vestige in Shakespeare's play of the unconsciously incestuous wooing of the daughter by the father which occurs in *Pandosto*. After the first act of *The Winter's Tale*, we could never have listened to a prolonged version of such a courtship with the required psychological innocence. Shakespeare turns the episode brilliantly (it is one of the few occasions on which Paulina is successfully snubbed):

Leontes.   . . . I'd beg your precious mistress,
    Which he counts but a trifle.
Paulina.   Sir, my liege,
    Your eye hath too much youth in't; not a month
    'Fore your queen died, she was more worth such gazes
    Than what you look on now.
Leontes.   I thought of her,
    Even as these looks I made. (V. i. 222-7)

Paulina, certainly, has not softened with the years. She plays remorselessly on Leontes' guilt, bringing it to the boil like a practised cook, and when Cleomones objects, turns on him with

> You are one of those
> Would have him wed again. (V. i. 23-24)

I suppose anyone in the audience who does not know that Hermione is living will side with Cleomenes here. Dion remonstrates most reasonably. But in reply Paulina is unmistakably authoritative, as she invokes the strange pagan gods of the play.

The assertive word 'pagan' may offend readers who like to Christianise the late Shakespeare. They might object that the plural 'gods' on which I hang my non-Christian interpretation is merely the result of the 1606 'Acte to restraine Abuses of Players'. This Act forbade the 'Abuse of the Holy Name of God in Stageplayes'[1] and meant, in effect, that the playwright could get away with writing 'gods', but not with 'God'. This seems at best a slender argument for emending 'gods' to 'God' wherever it occurs after 1606. No respectable textual scholar would look twice at it. In any case we have hardly leisure to speculate on the plays Shakespeare might have written under other conditions. The plays he actually wrote are difficult enough. *The Winter's Tale* speaks to us intermittently in Christian tones, but is certainly not univocally Christian. Hermione's use of the word 'grace' in Act I scene ii obviously owes something to the Christian development of the concept, but the theological context is several times removed. Polixenes at I. ii. 74 refers to Original Sin, but in a manner which looks like unconscious blasphemy. Shakespeare may indeed wish us to note this element of wildness in Polixenes' words yet the innocence for which Polixenes is fighting ultimately prevails in the scene against all the currents of feeling which oppose it. Paulina uses the language of Christianity when she calls Leontes a heretic at II. iii. 114. But if we take her language seriously we must conclude that Hermione is a Holy Martyr. In fact it is perfectly obvious that Paulina is speaking metaphorically at this point. But the description of the holy isle of Delphos falls with a quite different sort of weight. So also do many of the references to the gods:

> The gods themselves,
> Humbling their deities to love, have taken
> The shapes of beasts upon them . . . (IV. iv. 25-27)

> Besides, the gods
> Will have fulfill'd their secret purposes . . . (V. i. 35-36)

> You gods, look down,
> And from your sacred vials pour your graces

[1] The text of the Act is given in E. K. Chambers, *The Elizabethan Stage*, 1923, vol. IV, p. 338.

Upon my daughter's head! (V. iii. 121-3)

So again do the references to Nature:

> This child was prisoner to the womb, and is
> By law and process of great nature, thence
> Free'd and enfranchis'd . . . (II. ii. 59-61)

> . . . thou, good goddess Nature, which hast made it
> So like to him that got it. . . (II. iii. 103-4)

> There is an art which, in their piedness, shares
> With great creating nature (IV. iv. 87-88)

The play is resonant with a sense of the supernatural, but this never hardens into Christian Doctrine.

Yet S. L. Bethell's Christian interpretation of the play in his *The Winter's Tale: A Study* is occasionally persuasive. He scores a debating point when he writes on page 13, 'I find it difficult to understand why certain writers are convinced that Shakespeare cannot have seriously held the dogmas of Christianity.' But the point is easily answered; we are not concerned with the religious views of Shakespeare the man (which are, in principle, historically ascertainable); we are concerned with what is presented in the plays. It is certainly no part of my thesis to argue that Shakespeare was an unbeliever.

I have tried to meet the Christian interpretation by the method of matching references. For the reader who finds this method too crudely mathematical, a more macroscopic line of approach is open. William Empson once wrote[1] that to give a Freudian account of *Alice in Wonderland* one had only to tell the story. Something similar might be done for the Christian account of *The Winter's Tale*. Let us try it: Leontes' nature suffers a fall; Hermione, the very incarnation of mercy and love, is made a sacrifice; but, the sacrifice performed, death is cheated of his victim; the resurrection of Hermione results in the redemption of Leontes. If we capitalise the initial letters of 'fall', 'incarnation', 'mercy', 'love', 'sacrifice', 'resurrection', 'redemption', some readers will find it even more impressive. In fact however it relies to a great extent on the fallacy of the undistributed middle (e.g. cats are quadrupeds, dogs are quadrupeds, therefore cats are dogs); Christ was the Redeemer, Hermione is a redeemer, therefore *The Winter's Tale* is Christian. I have given first

---

[1] *Some Versions of Pastoral*, 1950, pp. 270-1.

a straightforward instance of the fallacious syllogism, and followed it with a sort of loose parody (for such I take the pseudo-argument in question to be). To tighten it up (in a fashion which the loose conclusion really presupposes) we should end 'Therefore Hermione is Christ'. Remove the fallacious elements, and you are left with an analogy between the 'myth' of Christianity and the myth of *The Winter's Tale* which is much looser than the terminology at first suggested.

If, then, I describe the restoration of Hermione as a sort of miracle, it will be understood that I intend no persuasive definition. When the statue of Hermione is found to be a living woman, we are not, after all, asked to believe that she was ever really dead. The play asks us to swallow the most strained and unlikely of natural events, but, if we except the special authority of the Oracle, it requires of us no acceptance of any supernatural events. In *The Tempest* we must believe that Prospero is a magician. But Paulina is frankly presented as a theatrical manipulator. Yet in spite of this—or, in an oblique fashion, because of this—Paulina is a more alarming figure than Prospero. For Prospero controlling the spirits of air and water a concept is available; he is a magician. But Paulina, screwing up the emotions of the onlookers with all the mumbo jumbo of a fairground mystagogue, is ultimately far harder to classify. The application of the rhetorical techniques of a huckster to a situation of immense human and mythical gravity propels us into an unfamiliar region. We can almost hear Paulina rubbing her hands with zest as she prepares Leontes and the rest for the spectacle:

> It is requir'd
> You do awake your faith. Then all stand still:
> Or—those that think it is unlawful business
> I am about, let them depart. (V. iii. 94-97)

In one way the speech is nonsense since it is not as if Hermione were actually coming to life at this point. Yet the audience cannot relax into the easy cynicism of 'seeing through the charlatan' since the most beautiful and wonderful thing is happening before its eyes; Hermione who was lost is found; Leontes' broken heart is healed. So Paulina's language is not so much over-pitched as under-pitched.

Obviously none of this subtlety could obtain if Hermione had really died; if the miracle were a Miracle in the bluntest sense. It is sometimes thought that in an earlier version of the play Hermione, like her analogue in Greene's *Pandosto*, was allowed to die. There are two principal arguments for this, one internal, one external. At III. iii. 19f. Antigonus describes how he was visited by the ghost of Hermione. Since only dead persons can appear as ghosts, this episode, it is argued, must be a survival from the older version of the play. In fact, as has often been pointed out, the argument is inconclusive. Although Antigonus himself takes the apparition as evidence for Hermione's death (see III. iii. 41-42) he was under no strict obligation to do so. Not all Jacobean ghosts are spirits of the dead. According to Walton's *Life*, John Donne saw the ghost of his wife when she was still alive. The other argument is drawn from Dr. Simon Forman's description of the play as he saw it in 1611. His account makes no mention of the statue scene, but implies that the climax, as with *Pandosto*, lay in the reunion of father and daughter.[1]

What seems to emerge from this is that even if there was an earlier version of the play in which Hermione really died, there was never any version in which Paulina's speeches formed the introduction to a genuinely supernatural resurrection.

Indeed, the effect of transposing the scene into such terms is disastrous. The marvellous dramatic irony of Paulina's lines (the conjuror transcended by his trick) would be reduced to sub-dramatic vulgarity. As it is, we have a wonderful poetic transformation of language as Paulina moves from the cheaply theatrical supernatural to the immense natural miracle. The point of transition is marked by the beginning of my italics:

> Music, awake her; strike!
> 'Tis time; descend; be stone no more; approach;
> Strike all that look upon with marvel. Come!
> *I'll fill your grave up: stir, nay, come away:*
> *Bequeath to death your numbness; for from him*
> *Dear life redeems you.*

So much that is moving in this scene springs from essentially natural sources. The point at which Leontes is distressed by Hermione's wrinkles (V. iii. 27-29) would, presumably, have been lost in a supernatural resurrection. The miracle is a human miracle. Leontes, on discovering that the statue is a living woman, is given imagery of intimacy, of domesticity—almost, of the prosaic:

[1] Forman's account is given in the Arden Edition, pp. xxi-xxii.

> O, she's warm!
> If this be magic, let it be an art
> Lawful as eating. (V. iii. 109-11)

Overtly, he is talking about magic, but the imagery automatically allies itself with the preceding reference to Hermione's warmth. The effect is to suggest that Hermione is at once the great passion of Leontes' life and as familiar to him as his daily bread. In fact, these lines imply precisely the antithesis between nature and magic that I have been trying to frame.

It will be noticed that my account of the miracle of Hermione's restoration is, in one sense of the word, a defence of its realism. What I could never defend, of course, is its probability. Readers who identify realism and probability will naturally be puzzled by this.

In a way *The Winter's Tale* itself is all about this very question. It not only exemplifies, it also treats what is meant by the realistic and the probable. Northrop Frye has a brilliant analysis of this in an essay[1] which may appear at first sight to be opposed to my own assertion of the realism of the play. He contrasts the mimetic realism of the sculptor Julio Romano, who 'would beguile Nature of her custom, so perfectly he is her ape' (V. ii. 98-99) with the ballad-like implausibility of the play as a whole. The play does not only present the material for this contrast; it also virtually asserts the contrast itself. The supposed statue is praised with Renascence enthusiasm for eye-deceiving verisimilitude while the actual loss and recovery of Perdita and Hermione is repeatedly presented to us as almost ridiculously incredible:

> A sad tale's best for winter: I have one
> Of sprites and goblins. (II. i. 25-26)

> . . . Is all as monstrous to our human reason (V. i. 41)

> . . . such a deal of wonder is broken out within this hour,
> that ballad-makers cannot be able to express it (V. ii. 23-25)

> This news, which is called true, is so like an old tale that
> the verity of it is in strong suspicion. (V. ii. 27-29)

[1] 'Recognition in *The Winter's Tale*', printed in his *Fables of Identity*, New York 1963, pp. 107-118.

Like an old tale still, which will have matter to rehearse,
though credit be asleep ... (V. ii. 62-63)

That she is living,
Were it but told you, should be hooted at
Like an old tale ... (V. iii. 115-17)

Frye argues that the play is as unrealistic as the trumpery ballads
purveyed by Autolycus; I, that the play is realistic. But in fact I am in
almost complete agreement with Frye. The contradiction is resolved by
distinguishing two senses of 'realistic'. For Fry 'realism' is plausibility.
There is certainly nothing wrong with this use of the word but, equally
certainly, my own differs from it. For I, as I say, hold that the play is at
once realistic and wildly improbable. At the beginning of this study,
feeling in need of the support of a clear head, I turned to Aristotle.
Perhaps the same philosopher can help us here.

As is well known, Aristotle in his *Poetics* says that the sequence of
events in a play should be probable; so far, so dull. But he also says
(1461b) with a sudden kindling of intelligence, that a probable impossibility is to be preferred to an improbable possibility. The epigram
is revealing. It lets out the fact that though art must be continuously
probable, life, in principle always possible, is *not* invariably probable.
Thus, while sheer impossibility is, naturally, still confined to the world
of art, improbability becomes, paradoxically, a characteristic of life.
Of course, if we *define* 'probable' as 'like life' the position we have reached
is self-contradictory. But that is not at all what 'probable' ordinarily
means. Rather it means 'like *most* of life'. The paradox is, then, free from
self-contradiction. It might even be true.

So *The Winter's Tale* is not only un-Aristotelian in structure. It also
breaks the Aristotelian rule of Probable Impossible. For in it Shakespeare
does the opposite of what artists are supposed to do; he prefers the
improbable possible to the probable impossible; he does what life
occasionally does, what art (in Aristotle's view) should never do. Art
is reasonable, life is capricious. In *The Winter's Tale* Shakespeare succeeded
in giving his wildly improbable story the warmth of actual life; he
succeeded in giving it realism. This concept of realism is, after all,
perfectly respectable. If it makes sense to say, 'I see that it is very unlikely
that this would happen, but, if it did, what would it *really* be like?' then
my own use of 'realism' makes sense, for it is the same use of the word.

At I. ii. 431 Polixenes says to Camillo (of Leontes' jealousy) 'How should this grow?' Camillo replies

> I know not: but I am sure 'tis safer to
> Avoid what's grown than question how 'tis born.

At V. iii. 117 Paulina, similarly challenged, contents herself with the unanswerable reply, 'It appears she lives.' These replies, rightly understood, do not show the want of naturalism in the play. They may stress the unlikelihood of the events of the play *qua* events, but they have no authority over the play itself. Rather, since they are themselves a part of the play, they tend to increase its realism. One has only to imagine Lysander or Demetrius saying anything of the sort in *A Midsummer Night's Dream* to realise how foreign such language is to truly conventional, non-naturalistic drama. We may shrink from believing in the restoration of Hermione, but we cannot but believe those who express our incredulity before we are able to do so for ourselves. In this way Shakespeare conciliates our belief in the implausible. In this way the improbable-realistic becomes a viable dramatic form. It might be said that he triumphs over Aristotle by yielding to him, since it is by frankly granting the improbability of what he describes (and, more importantly, by making the very characters involved grant its improbability) that he makes his winter's tale credible.

It is the realism of *The Winter's Tale* that makes it a miracle play; that is, a play about a miracle. No one ever thinks of the events of *A Midsummer Night's Dream* as miraculous, because no one ever thinks of them as real. *The Winter's Tale* is not indeed like 'most of life'. It will therefore never satisfy the criteria we normally apply to nineteenth century novels. It is instead like something very rare and sweet. Most of us have never experienced anything so wonderful and never will, but Shakespeare shows us what it might be like if we did.

There are some critics who seem to find it difficult to believe that any play which is a rich structure of images should contain human beings as characters. Yet Shakespeare again and again shows how it can be done. Similarly, there will be some who will conclude from my assertion of the naturalism of the play that I am denying its status as myth. Of course, I have no such intention. The play reaches down into the recesses of our awareness of things, releasing both dark violence and over-riding beauty. Northrop Frye has noted the violence:

Leontes, unable to sleep, wonders if having Hermione burnt alive would not give him rest. Antigonus offers to spay his three daughters if Hermione is guilty, though he would prefer to castrate himself. Mamillius, whom Leontes thinks of as part of himself, becomes the victim necessary to save Leontes, and the exposing of Perdita is attended by a sacrificial holocaust.[1]

The beauty I could try to convey by indiscriminate quotation. But it seems better on the whole to send my reader back to the text. Remember only that it is the same Hermione who can say at one point (in Jacobean English, of course) 'I can't stand this child a minute longer; somebody take him' (II. i. 1f.) and at another

> You gods, look down,
> And from your sacred vials pour your graces
> Upon my daughter's head! (V. iii. 121-3)

Myth, indeed, is both the heart of the play and the point at which interpretative criticism is silenced. If *The Winter's Tale* were an allegory, the reader might legitimately demand an explication of its 'significance'. But myth resists such treatment, because it is both a self-evident and a mysterious thing; self-evident, because anyone can perceive it; mysterious, because no one can (at the literary level) explain it. There is still, however, one question to be asked. What is the connexion between this heart of myth and the realistic/implausible technique I have tried to analyse?

C. S. Lewis, in his *An Experiment in Criticism* (1961),[2] pointed out that the distinguishing feature of myth is its power to move us even when it is summarised 'in the first words that come to hand'. The bare 'story' of Orpheus and Eurydice has a potency which the bare 'story' of *Middlemarch* has not. Note that the presence or absence of mythical content does not of itself constitute a criterion of literary merit. Stevenson's *Dr. Jekyll and Mr. Hyde* is not, I suppose, as good a book as *Middlemarch*, but it has far more 'myth-quality'. This might be taken to imply that since Stevenson could hit upon stories which were intrinsically good,

---

[1] 'Recognition in *The Winter's Tale*', *Fables of Identity*, New York 1963, p. 112.

[2] Pp. 40-42.

and George Eliot excelled in the unfolding of a story in itself indifferent, George Eliot should have written *Dr. Jekyll and Mr. Hyde* from a plot provided by Stevenson.

But this (and here we come to the point) is obviously not the case. George Eliot's version would have been worse than Stevenson's. We may represent the situation diagrammatically by two axes; let myth be the horizontal axis; let moral insight, human understanding, wit, idiosyncratic imagination, be the vertical. It seems clear that a high score on the vertical axis is of little assistance to us in our progress along the horizontal. Now Shakespeare came late to myth. He brought to it an immensely developed—one is tempted to say a hypertrophied— 'vertical' talent. His genius was admirably adapted to the profound imaginative transformation of indifferent story-material. But the uncovering of a myth was a very different matter. It may well be that in his new task Shakespeare found himself hampered by the presence of enormous, but ultimately irrelevant, energies and powers. Shakespeare indeed, is an extreme example of the vertically developed playwright. Critics who compare him with Sophocles, or with the great dramatists of France (who continue into the present century a tradition of mythical drama) continually speak of the 'diffuse', or the 'centrifugal' genius of Shakespeare.

If Shakespeare wrote *Pericles*, we may regard it as his first attempt at the communication in dramatic form of romantic myth. It is possible to see the play as a first attempt to resolve the difficulties I have described. Shakespeare, one guesses, finding his sophistication irrelevant to the matter in hand, simply threw it away. The action becomes as loosely episodic as anything of Brecht's. The playwright who has given us a Lear and an Antony, now offers us the puerile archaism of 'moral Gower'. The attempt failed, and *Pericles*, save for a few passages of heart-tearing beauty (in which quite a different technique is at work) is not a good play. If you are Shakespeare, it is no good trying to forget that you are a master of language, learned in human depravity and glory. Somehow, he had to find a way of unleashing all his 'vertical' genius in a fashion which left the basic framework of the mythical 'tale' still vividly evident.

In *The Winter's Tale*, Shakespeare found his way. He wrote with a closeness of psychological perception which is surpassed only in his greatest tragedies, but this high realism is not there to enrich or deepen the basic story. Instead it is set in a sort of opposition to the weirdly unlikely tale of seeming death and restoration. The mind of the spectator is thrown to and fro between a civilised enjoyment of sophisticated drama and an alarming encounter with something much more ancient, simple and mysterious—with a boldly isolated myth.

Select Bibliography

Barber, C. L., *Shakespeare's Festive Comedy*, Meridian Books, Cleveland and New York, 1963. Note: it may seem perverse to include this book, which mentions *The Winter's Tale* only three times, in a select bibliography. I do so, first because two of the three allusions are of very great interest, secondly because I know of no better account of the festive ritual which lies behind Shakespearean comedy as a whole (and hence behind Act IV of *The Winter's Tale* in particular).

Bethell, S. L., *The Winter's Tale: A Study*, Staples Press, 1947.

Frye, Northrop, 'Recognition in *The Winter's Tale*', available in *Essays on Shakespeare and Elizabethan Drama: In Honor of Hardin Craig*, University of Missouri Press, 1962; also in Northrop Frye's *Fables of Identity: Studies in Poetic Mythology*, Harcourt, Brace & World, New York, 1963.

Kermode, Frank, *Shakespeare: The Final Plays*, British Council Pamphlet, 1963.

Knight, Wilson, *The Crown of Life*, Methuen, 1948.

Mahood, M. M., *Shakespeare's Wordplay*, Methuen, 1957.

Stewart, J. I. M., *Character and Motive in Shakespeare*, Longmans Green and Co., 1949.

Traversi, Derek, *Shakespeare: the Last Phase*, Hollis and Co., 1954.

Index